T0209438

Robert's Orchid

YVETTE FEURTADO

BALBOA.
PRESS

A DIVISION OF HAY HOUSE

Balboa Press books may be ordered through booksellers or by contacting:

Balboa Press
A Division of Hay House
1663 Liberty Drive
Bloomington, IN 47403
www.balboapress.com
1 (877) 407-4847

Print information available on the last page.

ISBN: 978-1-9822-1834-8 (sc)
ISBN: 978-1-9822-1836-2 (hc)
ISBN: 978-1-9822-1835-5 (e)

Library of Congress Control Number: 2018914725

Balboa Press rev. date: 01/16/2019

Contents

Introduction

Hello

At this precise moment in time, you are reading the introductory pages to this book because you or others close to you have suffered a loss and are looking for words of comfort or inspiration regarding how to move forward. Perhaps you're feeling overwhelmed with grief and despair in the core of your being. What do you do when your world suddenly falls apart, and your heart's broken into a million pieces? The future you envisioned with the departed person will never materialize; he or she is gone, and here you are, seemingly left behind to endure the pain and suffering of a loss that's forever. Where do you go from here? How do you find peace and move on to fulfill your own destiny?

These are difficult questions to answer when you are grieving and cannot see how to get through the present day, let alone the next day, week, or month that lies ahead. Many will advise you to seek counseling, group therapy, and other well-meaning healing modalities that can help you on your path. I agree these can be helpful; nonetheless, for healing to occur, you must travel a path that is often traveled alone, going inward to the heart and soul of your true being and healing from inside out. It is a spiritual journey, a journey within to the essence of who you truly are, not to a distant place, retreat, or facility for healing.

I share with you my story of healing and

spiritual awakening as I traveled from darkness into the light and journeyed within to heal and transform my life after my beloved son, Robert, returned home to the light—to the spirit world, or heaven, as we often call it—after fulfilling his destiny here on Earth. Many who have lost a loved one, whether a son, daughter, parent, spouse, close family member, or friend, understand the profoundness of loss and how it shatters your world into pieces. Your life will never be the same. You slowly sink into an abyss of darkness, sorrow, and despair. It is difficult to see beyond each passing day without your loved one. Each day is cloaked with more sadness, and at some point, you become despondent because you hurt so much you want to go home too. Yes, this is the reality of those who grieve the loss of a loved one, most often alone. After everyone goes home after the funeral has passed, we stay home in the reality of the moment, knowing, feeling, remembering, wishing things were different, and often asking, "Why? Why did this happen?"

Time passes, and life goes on, but the darkness, grief, and despair remain ever present, and it's difficult to break free. You just want to surrender and be. Yet each passing day you live this way, the spirit of the person who departed suffers too. We are all eternally connected both in the physical plane and in spirit. We must, at some point, break away from all these low-vibrational emotions and thought forms, freeing ourselves to fulfill our own destinies. That is why we are still here. In doing this, we also set free the spirits of our loved ones so they may continue their own spiritual evolution in the light.

Moving forward takes courage and self-love.

We are destined for much more than the pain and suffering we have and may continue to experience. You can transform your life step by step and be free. Yes, you can do it. Follow my journey. The simple changes I note transformed my physical, emotional, and spiritual state into a vibrantly healthy physical, emotional, and spiritual being of love and light, as it was meant to be. I now live in the moment, as today is all we have, with gratitude and thankfulness for the opportunity to fulfill my destiny with dignity, honoring all gone before me.

This book describes steps to help you transform your physical and emotional self. In the process, you will amazingly transform on a spiritual level, allowing all that is positive and healing to guide your daily life. I've used simple language to facilitate understanding, clarity, healing, and transformation. At the end of the book, I have listed resources should you desire or need more guidance to continue your healing journey. Lastly, know that you are not alone. Whether you are religious or agnostic, there are divine beings always ready to assist you. All you need to do is invoke their assistance. These divine beings (e.g., God, Jesus, the archangels) follow the law of free will and cannot assist unless you invoke their presence.

Peace be with you.

Moving
Forward

I received a call from my son's father early in the morning on August 1, 2014, and at that precise moment in time, my life changed forever.

I had been home for three weeks on vacation. My son and I had gone to Montego Bay, Jamaica, for our annual vacation together and had a great time. I'd felt heaviness in my heart, as I always did, as I left home to return to my overseas post in the Middle East. I had been in the US Foreign Service for sixteen years, and I was considering retirement, looking forward to being home and spending more time with my son and family.

The accident occurred in the early morning, and I received the call that no parent wants to receive. My coworkers helped get me organized and back home within twenty-four hours after I got the call. The trip back to the United States was dreadful, and I could barely keep myself together to complete the journey home, knowing what waited.

Grief is an overwhelming emotion; it fills your entire being with darkness and despair. The light from within slowly seeps away and fades, and there you are, feeling hopeless, with nowhere to go but within to find the answers to the questions that have been troubling you since the passing of your loved one. You will likely wonder, *Why do we die? Why did my loved one die before me?* The latter question was especially troubling me since my son obviously had been younger and living a vibrant life.

Why do some die tragic deaths, and others go quietly into the night? What happens after we die? These questions are not easy to answer. Nonetheless, they set me on a course to find what I believe to be the truth about death—not from a programmed and conditioned religious or scientific perspective but from knowledge and wisdom within my soul—with the assistance of God and divine beings of light guiding my path. Along my journey toward healing, I met many individuals who also had suffered losses, and they shared their stories. I read books with themes of death and near-death experiences; had an introduction to the term *lightworker*; and read the work of sages of our time, spiritual teachers who would help me understand death and prompt a renaissance of divine love and light within the core of my being.

I discovered that all happens in perfect, divine timing, including our births and, yes, our deaths. Our ancestors lived for hundreds of years, but the physical body inevitably succumbs to the aging process and dies. Yet our spirit is immortal. In death, regardless of how a person dies, before the physical body actually dies, the spirit leaves and is guided by divine light back to its original source, to the heavenly or spirit realm. The spirit knows the way. I found this knowledge comforting, and it made sense. Suffering is our own human miscreation. Death is the completion of our destiny for this lifetime. Our spirit is immortal and returns to the light, remaining pure and divine, untouched by what's occurred to the physical body.

If you grew up in a family that went to church or practiced a religious belief, you might remember hearing or learning about death and the notion that upon death, you go to heaven if you were good or hell if you were an awful person. This is a fear-based belief that is still practiced today. Before my son's death, I believed we lived on this earth—hopefully a good life filled with love, laughter, and peace—and then, as we aged, there would come a time when we died and went to heaven. I never in a million years would have thought my son would die before I did. I learned along the way from darkness into the light that death, while hard to accept, means you have fulfilled your destiny, and it is time for your spirit to return home to continue its spiritual evolution in the light. I know this is not what a grieving person wants to hear, particularly in the midst of the recent loss of a loved one. I rejected this same statement. I imagine you are probably saying, "What on earth is she writing about, and how does she know?"

I know because after my son died, in the midst of my grief, his spirit visited me many times to let me know he was well. At first, I did not see, know, or acknowledge his spirit's presence because I was busy crying and feeling sad or numb from the loss, but his spirit, in an interesting way, revealed itself as the energy that we truly are and captivated my attention once I started listening to my intuitive sense. My son's spirit energy began communicating with me by tapping and drumming through the refrigerator, and at times, in lucid moments of tranquility, I would ask, "Robert, is that you making sounds through the refrigerator?" His spirit was persistent. The response would be a rhythmic tapping, as if he were physically there drumming on the refrigerator door. I would then let his spirit know how much I loved and missed him.

These occurrences continued for some time, and once I was able to move beyond the profound sadness I was feeling, other opportunities came my way to visit with his spirit in the heavenly realms through what are known as out-of-body experiences. We all have the ability to travel out of body and can do so when sleeping at night or napping during the day. When you awaken from sleep, you might think that it was just a dream or that you saw an image of a loved one, but you might have actually visited the heavenly realms. I know this might sound strange, but it is my truth. Once I opened myself up to what almost seemed unimaginable, my son's spirit helped me remember that I too am divine energy living in a physical body and manifesting my destiny on Earth.

This remembrance helped me understand his death. He died at age thirty-one in a tragic accident. I still say this sadly but now know that his destiny, planned before his birth, had been fulfilled.

We do not remember planning for the lives we will live on Earth or why death might be planned at such a young age. How we will die will always be unknown, but it is all part of the divine plan for our lives on Earth. It was difficult for me to grasp the profound significance of these few sentences, but with knowledge, understanding, and time spent in the heavenly realms with my son and divine beings of light, I now know the truth: our lives on Earth are planned before our birth, and so is our time to return to the heavenly realms.

The Rising Tide

After more than seven weeks away from work, it was time for me to resume employment activities. I did not return overseas. I was reassigned to Washington, DC, which allowed me at least to be close to a few friends and family. It was difficult to reengage with the flow of work and life that had been familiar before the loss. Days seemed endless and meaningless, with brief moments of tranquility. As each day progressed, emotions would surface. I'd remember all that had transpired and slowly slip into a state of sadness and despair.

There comes a time when you must answer these questions: "What happens now? How do I move on?" You are left to figure out what's next. Your loved one is gone; all the plans you made together have vanished. I decided it was time to go ahead and retire from the Foreign Service, as I had been planning before my son passed. I retired ten months after my son returned home to the spirit realm.

I was heartbroken. Life was truly different. I took on a few projects, but none materialized because I had not taken time to focus on what was really important: healing and understanding death. I am not speaking of death as many learn about it from a religious perspective while growing up. It was time to go within and heal from the inside out.

My starting point on the path of healing involved journaling and continued prayer. Interestingly, Reiki came into my sphere of awareness, and without hesitation, I signed up to learn Usui Reiki, an energy-healing modality that has helped me immensely throughout the last four years to heal on physical, mental, and emotional levels. Although there are other similar healing modalities, I encountered Reiki a few months before my son passed away—I remember this specifically—and know it was not a coincidence.

We must understand that moving forward with life after the loss of a loved one is challenging. You might digress many times before settling into a natural rhythm once again, reengaging, and enjoying simple activities of life.

It takes daily effort to avoid the pitfalls of sadness and despair or loathing life because your loved one is gone. Nonetheless, you must try and keep trying until the road less traveled becomes easier and bearable. One day, as you move forward on the path of healing, you will wake up and feel light, balance will be restored, and joy will return to your life.

Honor your loved one by moving onward and fulfilling your own destiny with dignity and a heart full of love for yourself and all who have gone before you. The love you shared will remain throughout eternity. To honor my son, Robert, I set up spaces around the house with photos of him—pictures of joyful and special moments to remind myself of happy times together. I look at these photos today not with sadness but with a remembrance of joyful moments. He is gone but never forgotten. It was hard at first, but with time, knowing that his spirit is free and at peace, I advance on my path of healing and restoring balance and joy in my life.

You too can do something similar to honor your loved one. Gather photos of happy moments, and place them in a photo album or in frames around the house. Start a garden or plant a tree in your loved one's honor. Pick up a hobby, something you've always wanted to do. Do something as remembrance to honor your loved one and the path you are on toward healing and restoration.

Time will slip by quickly, yet as you heal, each day will be a tribute to your loved one's life and your legacy as a resilient being of love and light. Start wherever you are, and do not look back. The past is just that—the past. There is no way to change what has occurred; just know that your loved one's spirit has returned home, no matter his or her lifestyle or how he or she lived life. It is not for us to judge others' character or actions. We all return to the heavenly realm and do a life review in which we understand the lessons of each opportunity, action, and life experience. There is no punishment. The harsh religious belief that we go to heaven or hell based on how we live our lives is not the case. So-called judgment is a life review, and you are your own judge. The review allows you to understand the opportunities gone by that you did not take and learn the lesson of each experience. This might sound too good to be true, but it is the truth I know. We need not fear death and the ultimate judgment by God, as we learned at a young age, because God is love, and love is what remains throughout eternity.

Begin your journey toward healing now. Let

the love and light of your true being surface and gently enfold you, filling your life again with hope, joy, faith, restoration, forgiveness, peace, and tranquility. It is a choice you must make; no one can do this for you. Move forward. The spirit of your loved one will rejoice, be at peace, and help you along the way.

Healing Your Physical Body

There was a time when humans lived for hundreds of years; this is recorded in history books, the Bible, and other publications. Our ancestors lived long lives in part because their diet consisted of natural foods, such as vegetables, fruits, and nuts from the earth, with no preservatives, additives, or modifications. These natural foods nourished and sustained their physical bodies.

As you move forward on the path of healing and transformation, it is necessary to look at what you are eating and drinking, as these elements of daily living affect you physically and emotionally. Pause for a moment to think about what you ate yesterday. Were the meals healthy? How did you feel afterward? Old habits, patterns and conditioning, the media, and other sources influence our eating habits, and when we are hurting emotionally, we gravitate toward eating as a pacifying behavior. I gained a lot of weight when in Washington, DC, during the final months of employment before I retired.

Now is the time to consider a different approach and change what you consume in order to regain your health and vitality for the next phase of life. Consider the following steps with an open mind. All are equally important, and each will assist you on your path of healing and transformation.

1. Detoxify your body. Look for a detox program that is plant-based, with no chemicals or preservatives, and does not impede your daily activities. You might want to consider juicing as another option rather than an off-the-shelf detox, yet whatever you choose, detoxifying your physical body is the starting point toward health and wellness. Consult with your physician if you think it's necessary.

2. Clean out your pantry. Eliminate all products that have preservatives; artificial additives, flavors, or coloring; or MSG and any genetically modified organisms (GMOs). The preservatives and artificial flavors, etc., are harmful and can cause disease and illness.

3. Eliminate meat from your diet. When you eat meat, you are eating dead flesh. Think about this for a moment. Furthermore, it takes a lot of effort for the body's digestive system to process meat, and meat consumption affects your health. (Consult with a physician regarding cholesterol, triglycerides, and blood sugar.) Your best option in terms of nutrition is to eat fresh, raw vegetables and fruits and fill your refrigerator and cupboards with protein-rich foods. This might be challenging, but you can do it. It is part of a lifetime commitment to eating healthfully. Once you adjust to this and other changes in your diet, you will be thankful for taking on this challenge. You will feel lighter, and

your body will appreciate the efforts made toward wellness.

4. Eat wholesome foods. Opt for almond or almond-coconut milk; brown rice; sweet potatoes; pasta made of protein, brown rice flour, or sprouted grains; fruits; nuts; and copious amounts of fresh vegetables. Eating organic food is preferable.

5. Stop drinking alcoholic beverages. Alcohol weakens the immune system, damages vital organs, and is a depressant.

6. Drink lemon water (with no sugar or additives) first thing in the morning before eating breakfast and throughout the day if possible. Squeeze half a lemon into four ounces of warm water—it should be almost hot to the touch—and drink slowly. Wait at least ten to fifteen minutes before eating.

Lemon water energizes your digestive system, liver, and pancreas and helps with detoxing.

7. Drink alkaline water. Have yourself tested to determine your pH value. Your pH should be 7 or above. There are commercial brands of bottled water that offer pH-balanced water, or consider purchasing a water filtration system. Drink lots of water, and eliminate all beverages that have any type of processed sugar or flavor additives.

8. Go outdoors, and enjoy being out in the sun to ensure your body produces the required vitamin D it needs to support your immune system, bones, and teeth. The sun's energy and light will revitalize your being. Ten to fifteen minutes of direct sunlight will do.

9. Exercise every day. Make an effort each day to do this. This activity has always been a lifesaver for me. Exercise activates endorphins in your body—feel-good hormones that can help uplift you, especially when you are feeling sad. Exercise can be a simple fifteen- to twenty-minute walk twice a day. You should exercise for a minimum of thirty minutes per day. It really does the body good to exercise daily. I walked almost every day while in DC, and thankfully, I had a walking buddy with whom I could share how I was feeling and chat about life and work. In inclement weather, you can go to a gym, invest in an exercise DVD, or watch TV or listen to music while you walk in place. There are many options available

when weather does not permit outdoor activity.

10. Decalcify your pineal gland. Your pineal gland, also referred to as the third eye, is a small endocrine gland in the center of your brain. It produces chemicals and hormones—such as serotonin and melatonin—that cause happiness, serenity, restfulness, and balanced emotions, which are natural states of being for all humans. A calcified pineal gland is the result of lack of proper nutrition, left-brained thinking, chemicals, and environmental issues. All of us want to return to our natural state of being. Below are a few suggestions to incorporate into your daily living to help decalcify your pineal gland.

- Eliminate fluoride from your household. Fluoride is found in toothpaste, mouthwash, and tap water. Fluoride is a poisonous chemical toxic to the human system.

- Reduce the acidity in your body by eliminating, at a minimum, beef and pork from your diet.

- Drink alkaline water, and eat more green vegetables, which are alkaline rich and charged with sunlight.

- Go outside to spend time in the sun (without sunglasses), and look up at the beautiful sun to reenergize.

If you have reservations about decalcifying the pineal gland, look further into this subject. There is a wealth of information available regarding the pineal gland. Do what's best for you and your family.

11.Practice earthing every day. Earthing refers to making direct contact with the surface of the earth (i.e., walking barefoot on the grass). In doing this every day for as long as possible, you will receive a charge of the earth's energy, which promotes health and wellness. This is a simple yet highly effective method of reenergizing your being naturally with no side effects.

Once you detoxify, modify what you consume each day, and follow what's noted above, your body will feel much better. You will feel reenergized, and your emotions will stabilize.

Calm the Mind

Listening to the voice within, your intuition, is difficult when you are grieving the loss of a loved one. It's hard to focus on the positive aspects of life when all you want to do is curl up on the sofa or in bed and cry. Your mind repeats the same messages of sadness and despair over and over again until you can summon the courage and determination to say, "Enough!" and decide it's time to move on. Moving on does not mean forgetting what has happened; it means living again by remembering that your loved one has fulfilled his or her destiny and returned home, as planned before he or she was born. In living again, you honor your loved ones and allow their spirits to be at peace. They will love you forever for letting go and moving on.

I understand these words are hard to accept, especially if you've just suffered a loss, but know that you picked up this book for a reason. Your inner voice, your intuition, is nudging you. It knows it's time to reengage with life and move forward. Listen to it. Be gentle with yourself, and do not retreat into darkness, which will only prolong the inevitable realization that your loved one is physically gone, and there is nothing you can do to change that. You must forge ahead with inner knowingness that your loved one's spirit has returned to a place of peace and love, and you will join him or her one day when you too have fulfilled your destiny.

Meditation will help you calm the mind, and as you practice, you'll be able to quiet and release all that keeps you anchored to low-vibrational thoughts and emotions, such as sadness, grief, anger, and fear. Meditation can help you achieve mental clarity and an emotionally calm state of being. There are many techniques for meditation. If you want to keep it simple, consider the following technique. Sit in a chair cross-legged or, if you desire, lie down on your bed. Set your intent to quiet the mind, close your eyes, and take deep breaths with your mouth closed, breathing in and out through the nose. Breathe into the belly, and let out each breath slowly and gently. At first, and perhaps for many sessions, it will be difficult to quiet all the repetitive thoughts and emotions that may surface. Let it be, and let it all go. Refocus your attention on your deep breathing. The goal is to quiet the mind—no thoughts and no emotions, just breathing and a clear and calm mental state. It takes a lot of practice, but you can do it. Keep trying, and one day it will click. Be gentle with yourself. There is no set destination you must reach. The goal is to have calmness, peace, serenity, and quietness each day as you move forward and restore balance in your being.

Find a meditation technique that resonates with you. If you have any reservations about it, look online or in a bookstore, or chat with a family member or friend who practices meditation.

Lastly, during your quiet moments, incorporate soft, gentle, healing music to help move you along with the healing process. Try listening to solfeggio-frequency music for physical and emotional healing. The solfeggio frequency is gentle and comforting. I also found Stephen Halpern's music and crystal and Tibetan singing-bowl music to be comforting as well.

Revitalize Your Energy Flow

In the midst of processing all that has happened, you might lose track of the last time you ate a healthy meal, bathed, washed your hair, or just breathed deeply and relaxed. Your emotional being might remain in a state of shock, and as a result, blockages in your energy flow might develop from the physical, mental, and emotional turmoil you are experiencing. Thoughts, feelings, and possible side effects of suffering can manifest in your physical body.

How do we return to a natural state of mental, physical, and emotional harmony after the loss of a loved one? This is a challenging endeavor. There will be days when you manage to find your balance and go about your day with tranquility and ease. On other days, the longing and sadness will reappear, and suddenly, you will find yourself crying and reexperiencing the emotional turmoil once again by remembering what has happened. This learned repetitive process is the issue you must address firsthand. Meditation is a key factor in calming the mind and bringing in a heightened state of awareness whereby you are cognizant almost immediately of these paralyzing thoughts and have the choice to stop their manifestation as they surface. It is not difficult or impossible to do. You must empty your mind of that which causes suffering. We must learn to detach ourselves from thoughts, patterns, and emotional behaviors that keep us in a low-vibrational state and develop new patterns and behaviors that will lift us as we process what has happened and move forward on the path of healing and transformation.

In order to heal our mental, physical, and emotional states of being, it's necessary to address the energy system in our bodies through which our life-force energy flows and the impact of blockages and imbalances that may occur as a result of loss, trauma, or other circumstances in our lives. Interestingly, we do not learn about the vital energy system within our bodies that keeps us mentally, physically, emotionally, and spiritually healthy.

Noted below is a simple description of our

primary energy centers, most notably called chakras, which are located along the midline of the body from the base of the spine to the crown of the head.

- *The base (or root) chakra.* This first chakra is located at the base of the spine. It is considered the center of security and stability. The color associated with this chakra is red.

- *The sacral chakra.* This second chakra is located just below the navel. It is considered the center of emotions, creativity, and sexuality. The color associated with this chakra is orange.

- *The solar-plexus chakra.* This third chakra is located above the navel. It is considered the center of will and personal power. The color associated with this chakra is yellow.

- *The heart chakra.* This fourth chakra is located over the center of the sternum. It is considered the center of love and compassion. The color associated with this chakra is green.

- *The throat chakra.* This fifth chakra is located in the throat area. It is considered the center of personal truth and communication. The color associated with this chakra is blue.

- *The third-eye chakra.* This sixth chakra is located in the middle of the forehead. It is considered the center of intuition and inspiration. The color associated with this chakra is indigo.

- *The crown chakra.* This seventh chakra is located at the top of the head. It is considered the center of spirituality and self-enlightenment. The color associated with this chakra is gold.

Many individuals are not aware or have not ever heard of energy centers or chakras, but they are the means by which our energetic, vital life force flows through our beings. Once you begin to consistently work on clearing any blockages and revitalize your energy flow, you will feel strong and uplifted and desire to continue your path of healing. This is a daily effort you must commit to. You will know when blockages have cleared from your energy centers. The chakras have their own rhythm; the energy flows in a clockwise motion.

I recommend you do this every day. Once the energy flow has been restored, continue this daily practice to remain in a state of balance. To find a good baseline to start at to clear any blockages in the energy system, go online to YouTube, visit a bookstore, or ask a friend. There are many options for chakra healing and balancing. I have used Deepak Chopra's *The Soul of Healing Meditations* and *Chakra Balancing: Body, Mind, and Soul* for a long time. It works for me. It's a simple approach. Dr. Chopra gives a brief introduction to the chakra system and uses a guided meditation format, an uncomplicated approach to this critical component of your healing. It's not a coincidence that I found his CD a few years ago before my son passed away and downloaded the CD's guided meditation and music onto my cell phone. There are many options available. Find what resonates with you the most, and move forward with this activity. One day soon, after consistently doing this, your energy centers will be restored to balance.

Letting Go

This is the greatest challenge you will undertake on the path of healing. You must do it. Be brave and courageous, and do not resist. Resisting only prolongs your suffering.

Let's be clear: you are letting go of the grief, sadness, guilt, anger, and other low-vibrational emotions and thought forms that keep you in a state of despair. You must summon the courage and self-love from within to move forward into the light of your true being and reignite a spark that will take you on a new path, a different direction to fulfill your destiny. This new path is filled with love, peace, harmony, and joy. It is how life is meant to be. You will keep all the beautiful memories of times gone by with your loved one; they are etched in your soul for eternity.

When you allow yourself to let go, your life will take on a fresh meaning that will reenergize you and help you see life in a different way. Yes, life will be different. The past is behind you. You lived, loved, and did what you were meant to do when your loved one was physically with you. Now the wave of change has come. Flow with it. Move gently into the future you planned long ago before you were born. Trust yourself and your intuition, the inner knowingness that surfaces to guide you each day. Because of our busy lives, we often don't acknowledge the intuitive sense we all have, but it is there within. What is it saying to you as you read these words?

You must want to let go and heal. It is your choice, and no one can do it for you. The time will come. What will you choose? It is a choice you must make in the not-too-distant future, after some time has passed and you have fully realized what has happened and understand that the death of your loved one was planned for a set time. The how is always an unknown factor. This statement is not meant to make you sad or angry or evoke an emotional reaction; it just is. You must ask yourself, "Where do I go from here?"

Healing will occur at your own individual pace. Do not feel rushed by anyone or any other event occurring in your life as you read this book. Healing from grief is a personal effort. Take your time. There is no set destination you must reach. Move gently, one day at a time.

I began writing in a journal a few weeks after

my son passed. I could not bear the loss; my pain was too profound. I descended into an abyss of hopelessness. My family was not very helpful, as they too were dealing with the loss of their nephew and other losses they had not taken time to heal. My extended family and friends reached out, but they too carried their own unhealed emotions of past losses and therefore were not fully available to help me through my own process. Nevertheless, I do appreciate their efforts to reach out. It might seem as if I were alone, but my God is a merciful God who sends divine intervention my way. To this day, four-plus years after my son returned home to the spirit world, I feel the love of divine beings with me always, and for this, I am eternally grateful.

As I noted above, I started a journal, and I made entries about how I was feeling almost every day.

The darkness within revealed itself in the words I wrote. That was the start of my own healing process. Writing down my thoughts helped, as there wasn't anyone I really trusted to share the depth of what I was feeling. Some of you might have a trusted family member or friend, and it is wonderful if you do. Please share your thoughts and feelings; it will help you. As I made journal entries, many life lessons became clear with each passing day. I did not deliberately plan to learn those lessons as I wrote, but the lessons I was to learn in this lifetime from loss and grief came up. While writing, I'd suddenly have an epiphany and understand the life lesson. You too will have moments like this if your heart is open to all the lessons the experience of loss offers to those left behind.

Begin where you are at in this moment in time.

Begin your own journal, and let the words flow. Healing will follow slowly. It too has a rhythm of its own. As you step into the light each day, engage in gentle activities that nurture you. I recommend taking a few weeks off from work if possible and communing with nature. If weather permits, go for long walks in a park, by a lake, or at the beach. The flow of energy from nature is soothing; it will help bring calm, and if you close your eyes momentarily and allow yourself to just be, you are able to enter into a state of peace and tranquility as you move forward with your healing journey.

There are other gentle activities you can consider undertaking, such as coloring. Yes, coloring. In today's world, it's called adult coloring. I spent many hours coloring. A friend sent me an adult coloring book for Christmas a little more than a year after my son passed. I spent countless hours coloring as part of my individual therapy. It's a calming activity, and using colors is therapeutic as well. The natural colors of red, orange, yellow, green, blue, indigo, violet, and white have special vibrations that correspond with the seven energy centers mentioned in the "Revitalize Your Energy Flow" section and can help activate your energy centers and promote healing. The color white, while not part of the energy-center color scheme, has the highest vibration of all colors. I wore black for more than a year after my son died—a useless cultural tradition that permeates darkness. Black is a low-vibrational color. Had I known what I know now—that white carries a higher vibration—I might have opted to wear white instead. I don't wear black anymore.

My point about color and its effects is this:

consider stepping away from religious, family, and mainstream culture and traditions as they relate to death and funerals. Such traditions cloak you in darkness and keep you in a low-vibrational state of being. Free yourself to move forward on the path of light. Other calming and peaceful activities include painting; writing music; listening to gentle, healing music (listen to all nine solfeggios, a healing frequency of music—you can find several selections on YouTube—or listen to Steven Halpern's music); gardening; and meditating. These activities nurture your being.

Healing with Crystals

As I moved forward with transforming my life after the loss of my son, there were days when all seemed to fall into place, with peace and serenity at the forefront of every effort on the path of light. Some days I digressed and found myself in a state of sadness. Emotions would pop up out of nowhere.

Two years ago, healing with crystals came into my sphere of awareness. I was browsing in a bookstore one weekend, when a book on healing with crystals came into view, and I intuitively knew I had to buy the book and take it home. That was how I discovered this interesting approach to healing, all in divine timing.

Crystals are natural solids made from minerals and are formed in the earth's surface. They have been used for healing since ancient times. How do crystals work? Crystals work through the human energy system (see the information on chakras in the section "Revitalize Your Energy Flow"), not through the physical body. Crystals channel energy that can help with physical, mental, and emotional healing and spiritual development.

I went through the entire book the same evening, learning about crystals. Each has general, physical, emotional, and spiritual healing qualities. It sounds unreal, but it's true. I have used many in my own healing process since discovering this approach, and I use them consistently during meditation. I carry a few with me all the time—rose quartz, schungite, and rainbow fluorite—and I sleep with a few that I place in a pouch and keep in my pocket or on my night table. I have created crystal grids around my home to bring and maintain positive energy. The energy in the home space can become stale and lack flow as a result of the mourning process and empty spaces that previously were filled with joy and laughter when your loved one was physically with you and life flowed happily. You need to refresh those spaces. Crystals can help bring positive energy into your being and home.

I made a list of all the crystals I thought I needed, with a focus on revitalizing my energy centers and clearing low-vibrational emotions and thought patterns. Our emotions and thought patterns keep us in a state of hopelessness and despair; therefore, the intent of crystal use is to slowly and gently transform how we feel and think by using a natural approach, not chemicals, medication, or sedatives, which give us momentary relief without addressing the core issues we need to heal.

There has been divine timing in all that has transpired in my life since my son returned home to the spirit world, and finding a small crystal shop in the heart of a flea market close to my hometown the weekend after I purchased the book was no exception. Finding the small shop was timely, and I purchased the crystals needed to help me heal and transform. I could have found all the crystals I needed online, but there is something special about holding a crystal in your hand and connecting with it before buying it. With online shopping, you cannot hold the crystal until after you have purchased it and had it delivered to your home.

As noted above, I carry, wear, and sleep with crystals and have crystal grids throughout my home. Even if you are skeptical about using crystals, give yourself the opportunity to at least try this interesting approach to healing. The key is to open your mind to the possibility. The intent is to focus on using the crystals to help with healing your energy centers. Incorporate crystals that will complement the physical, emotional, and mental healing process. Along the way, you will be uplifted spiritually, rediscovering the true essence of your being.

Below, I list crystals that can help revitalize your energy centers, or chakras, and a few that helped me with clearing low-vibrational emotions and thought patterns. Many crystals can help; find those that resonate with you. These are just recommendations. Once you start looking at individual crystals, you'll be surprised at the amazing healing qualities each has to help you heal. Please remember that crystals help with the healing process; none can heal you on its own.

- *Shungite* . Shungite helps with purifying your body. It helps to clear your body of any dysfunctional patterns, which can manifest as negativity and emotional difficulties. Place the stone above the root chakra when meditating, and wear it every day. Tape it above your root chakra. If that's impractical, then at a minimum, carry it with you. Its color is black.

- *Apache tear.* This stone helps with emotional balance, forgiveness, and overcoming negativity and grief. Place it above the root chakra when meditating, and carry it with you. Its color is black.

- *Rose quartz.* This quartz has calming qualities and helps with forgiveness, love, romantic relationships, and overcoming grief. Place it above the heart chakra when meditating, and wear it or carry it with you. Its color is rose, or pink.

- *Smoky quartz.* This quartz helps with negativity, anger, depression, despair, and grief. Place it above the root or sacral chakra when meditating, and carry it with you. Its color is deep to light brown.

The Shungite, Apache tears, rose quartz, and smoky quartz assist with grief and the release of negative emotions and thought forms that keep you in a low-vibrational state of being. As you move forward in coming to terms with what has occurred, be gentle with yourself, and know deep within that your loved one has transcended the physical world, is continuing his or her own evolution as a spirit in the higher realms, is at peace, and wishes you peace too. Rise from the disheartening situation you are in. Move—run— toward the path of light.

The seven crystals noted below will help you with chakra healing, clearing, tuning, and balance. Beyond helping to clear blockages in your energy system, each has individual healing qualities. The use is simple: just place each above the specific chakra area when meditating. Lying down will facilitate the placement and stability of each crystal. Use all the crystals when doing a guided meditation to clear your chakras. Carry them with you to draw in their energy, or wear them. There are no side effects to worry about. Your being will appreciate the natural and pure energy from the crystals.

- Use red jasper, hematite, or garnet to help heal, clear, tune, and balance the root chakra.
- Use carnelian, smoky quartz, or bloodstone to help heal, clear, tune, and balance the sacral chakra.
- Use citrine, yellow quartz, or tiger's-eye gold to help heal, clear, tune, and balance the solar-plexus chakra.

- Use malachite, green aventurine, or rose quartz to help heal, clear, tune, and balance the heart chakra.

- Use blue lace agate, blue calcite, or angelite to help heal, clear, tune, and balance the throat chakra.

- Use lapis lazuli, sodalite, or celestite to help heal, clear, tune, and balance the third-eye chakra.

- Use an amethyst, clear quartz, or selenite to help heal, clear, tune, and balance the crown chakra.

Moments
in Time

If tomorrow starts without me, tell her I loved her more than I could express. Tell them I lost my way, and God showed up to walk me home.

—Robert E. Feurtado

I found these words written on a piece of paper a few months after my son passed away. Heartbroken and grieving, I believed he left this message to let me know he loved me and was safe within the warm embrace of our Father-Mother God.

I stapled the piece of paper to my journal, and it has been almost four years since I last laid eyes on it. As I reread this note, tears flowed. This will happen from time to time. Written words, songs, places, and precious moments shared with your loved one will remain etched in your soul forever.

Divine
Assistance

This is a touchy subject; however, in writing my personal story, I would be remiss if I did not mention the divine assistance I have received and continue to receive daily on my path toward healing and wholeness. I understand that some people around the world do not believe in God or divine beings of light who are always with and around us every day. There is no judgment one way or another.

My healing journey has been divinely inspired,

and as I live each day, my being is filled with gratefulness beyond words for the assistance I receive from God, Jesus, the angelic kingdom, and other divine beings of love and light. My purpose in writing these few words is not to convince you of their existence or their presence in your life. They are there, standing by, waiting for your call for help. All divine beings follow the law of free will and cannot assist unless you invoke their presence. You need not belong to a religion, cult, or sect to pray or invoke their presence in your life. Simply say, "Please help me, God," "Please help me, Jesus," or "Please help me, Buddha," or use the name of another divine being.

Yes, it is that simple and uncomplicated. You are not required to have a religious affiliation or join a church or congregation of any kind. There is no contract or obligation, just appreciation for the help they provide.

There are many archangels, such as Michael and Gabriel, who are mentioned in the Bible and other religious texts. They can also provide assistance in healing specific areas and issues in your life beyond the grief and sadness you are experiencing. These beautiful, divine beings are not affiliated with a specific religion; therefore, anyone can invoke them anywhere and at any time. It is important to note that the archangels also follow the law of free will and cannot assist unless you invoke their presence. Invoke their assistance by saying, "I invoke the assistance of Archangel _____," and then state what you need assistance with. Below, I list a few archangels who have helped me along the way; however, there are many more. Take the time to research beyond what's noted below so you can get the assistance you need.

- Archangel Michael: Michael is the leader of all the archangels and is a powerful protector; all who call upon him are safe from harm.

- Archangel Chamuel: Chamuel is the archangel of pure love and helps with healing grief and depression.

- Archangel Jeremiel: Jeremiel can help us to review our lives while we're still living and correct wrongs we've done and make changes needed in our lives.

- Archangel Raphael: Raphael is a powerful healer and can assist with physical and spiritual healing.

- Archangel Zadkiel: Zadkiel can help with forgiveness for yourself or someone else and assist with letting go of judgment of self and others.

I found the Hawaiian Ho'oponopono prayer helpful as well. It can be used to ask for forgiveness of living and deceased family and friends.

Don't Forget the Children and Young Adults

After the death of a loved one, children and young adults suffer too and possibly will be confused about what has happened. They might be fearful of what's to come next, particularly if the loss was of a parent; a sibling; another close relative, such as a grandparent or auntie; or a friend. Be gentle with them; they will need lots of nurturing and love. Seek counseling from a kind and compassionate grief counselor who specializes in helping children and young adults through the grief process. Kindness and compassion are key.

Take time to sit with your children or young adults and, as gently as possible, explain what has happened. They deserve to hear the truth and to know that death is the completion of a destiny fulfilled and a return to the spirit world, heaven, where we come from originally, as a divine spirit spark of our God. If you are agnostic, that's okay. Explain what has occurred in a gentle manner that will alleviate any fears they might have about death. Openly communicating and sharing information about this subject without fear will help them understand that death is the natural evolution of every human being.

Consider finding a grief counselor who

uses play, such as sand play; art; writing and journaling; or music in his or her counseling sessions. Children and young adults are not always inclined to have a conversation about how they are feeling; therefore, play, art, writing, and music might be good outlets for self-expression. Keep a close eye on them so they don't internalize the sadness they are feeling. It's important they have a way to express how they are feeling inside and understand how to let go and move forward without guilt, shame, anger, or a belief that the death of their loved one was somehow their fault. As a parent, grandparent, auntie, sister, brother, close or distant relative, or friend, whatever the case, look beyond your immediate needs related to dealing with the loss of your loved one to consider those in your sphere of awareness who might also need help, and reach out. At the end of the day, we are all one.

There are many resources that can help with the grief process. Seek help. Look online and within your community to find which resource will work best for you and your family.

Reaching Out and Helping Others

You have read through the pages of this book and understand the grief, pain, sorrow, and many daily challenges an individual can experience while grieving the loss of a loved one. Start your journey toward healing today. Do not linger in darkness and despair. Each day that you live on this beautiful earth is a gift. Live in the moment.

Today is all we have; therefore, find meaningful ways to bring peace into your life despite what has happened.

As you journey back to wellness, you will meet others who have also suffered profound losses. Help them. Let your story and journey to wellness and transformation inspire all you meet in the humblest and most meaningful way. As you meet others who are suffering, reach out, stay in touch, and be a guiding light in their darkness.

After the funeral and burial of my son, many said, "I'll be in touch," "I'll stop by to visit soon," or "Call if you need to talk," but most moved on, and while grieving, I did not want to speak with anyone over the phone. I say this to make the following point: if you say any of the phrases noted above, mean it, and do it. Otherwise, it's okay to just express condolences and move on with your life. Try your best not to overcommit to a follow-up visit or phone call if, in your heart, you know it might not happen. Life does go on, but the lives of the deceased's mother, father, sister, brother, close relatives, and friends have changed forever, and they need the extended support of relatives, friends, and even acquaintances during this difficult period. Mean what you say at all times, and follow through. Doing so will keep everything real and in perspective.

If you do call, text, or email to inquire how one is doing, know that the person appreciates the gesture even if there is no immediate response. Remember, the pain of loss is devastating. The shock and other emotions take time to heal. The individual might read your message or see the call on caller ID but be unable, due to the emotional turmoil, to have a conversation or reply. Do not be upset or take it personally. Keep trying, and the person will appreciate your efforts. One day in the not-too-distant future, he or she will be the one calling, texting, or emailing to say thank you for the words of encouragement and efforts to stay in touch.

As you move forward with your healing journey, let the knowingness within you, your intuition, guide you, and allow yourself to be transformed. It will be a life different from the one you envisioned, but that is how it was meant to be. Honor the past and your loved one by living a life that matters and living up to your full potential, your destiny.

Transcend the Path of Sorrow

I am writing this final section of the book exactly four years and one month after the death of my son. In real time, I will always miss him and his gentle spirit, yet I feel a sense of peace as I continue my journey. I want to share with you an experience I had just a few weeks ago that led to my writing this section. My recent experience again confirmed without a doubt that our spirits are immortal. While the physical body returns to the earth, the spirit lives on throughout eternity.

I was in Hawaii, attending the Thirty-Second World Congress on Illumination. A few days after the conference began, while I was eating lunch, I met a young lady and started a conversation about life and family. Unbeknownst to me, she had the ability to see spirits and channel messages. That is her special, divine gift. We all have special gifts that manifest in our lives when we are ready to use the gifts in service to the divine and humanity.

As our conversation progressed, she asked me if I had children, and I proceeded to share with her my story of love and loss of my only child. She did not blink. She asked how old my son had been when he passed and asked for a physical description. After I responded, she paused from eating for a few moments, looked at me, and said in the calmest and gentlest manner, "He is standing behind you and has a message for you."

She gave me a physical description of what he'd looked like at the age of thirty-one. He was healthy, strong, tall, and handsome and enjoying life. His message for me was succinct and beautiful. He said, as channeled through the young lady, "I am free, happy, and at peace. I want you to be happy and at peace too. I love you." He asked that I have a good day and return to Pearl Harbor on Oahu, Hawaii, which we'd visited together when he was about eight years old, and he asked that I enjoy an ice cream.

It was an extraordinary moment in time; my son's spirit was there with me at a vacation location we'd enjoyed long ago. Time, space, and distance were irrelevant. His spirit came forth to bring a message of hope, peace, and love, a remembrance that we are one. There is no separation, just a change of worlds, and love is all there is. His message, channeled through a stranger who became a lifelong friend, let me know his spirit was free, happy, and at peace. I wept, overwhelmed by emotion—but not sadness. I had a feeling of joy and peace combined with a sense of nostalgia.

I was meant to visit Pearl Harbor again. We had the afternoon free, so I made my way back to Pearl Harbor and spent the afternoon in quiet contemplation, thankfulness, and prayer, grateful for the experience and the knowingness that my son's spirit is well and lives on forever in the heavenly realms, surrounded by love and the gentle embrace of our Father-Mother God. I had ice cream that evening to honor my son and his request.

Believe you are more than a physical body here today and gone tomorrow. We were all created by a universal force beyond our comprehension and are embodied on earth at this precise moment in time to awaken and remember the true essence of our being. We are all divine spirits on earth, learning here in this lifetime to transcend old beliefs, programming, and conditioning that have kept us fearful of death and unaware of our divine nature and true purpose. Our real home lies beyond the stars. It is a realm of infinite possibilities where love, peace, and beauty are boundless, and it is where our spirits return once we have completed our lessons on earth and fulfilled our destinies.

Awaken, step beyond all old patterns of thinking, and believe you were destined for more than just life and death. We are eternal beings of love and light.

Pace Yourself

Speed in races …

in accomplishing tasks … and

in achieving goals … but

Pace yourself in life …

Too often do people look back

at time from a place they once

thought they wanted to be …

wondering where it all went …

not fully realizing that they were

there for however brief a time

but because of the rapid rate of

progression that they insisted upon,

the journey and best parts were missed

and lost in a blur … wishing for it back …

regretting …

Pace yourself, my friends … enjoy every

minute … let life be your perpetual journey

with each experience a new chapter in your

story.

—*Robert E. Feurtado*

Resources

Arienta, Sahvanna. *The Lightworker's Source.*

Bertoldi, Concetta. *Do Dead People Watch You Shower?*

Bertoldi, Concetta. *Inside the Other Side.*

Bodine, Echo. *Echoes of the Soul.*

Brinkley, Dannion, and Kathryn Brinkley. *Secrets of the Light (Lessons from Heaven).*

Burpo, Todd, and Sonja Burpo. *Heaven Changes Everything.*

Burpo, Todd, and Sonja Burpo. *Heaven Is for Real.*

De Angelis, Barbara. *Soul Shifts.*

Dooley, Mike. *The Top Ten Things Dead People Want to Tell You.*

Dyer, Wayne W., and Dee Garnes. *Memories of Heaven.*

Eaton, Barry. *Afterlife.*

Frazier, Karen. *Crystals for Healing.*

Hanh, Thich Nhat. *No Death, No Fear.*

Hay, Louise. *You Can Heal Your Life.*

Linn, Denise. *Past Lives, Present Miracles.*

Permult, Philip. *The Crystal Healer.*

Schwartz, Robert. *Your Soul's Plan.*

St. John of the Cross. *The Dark Night of the Soul.*

Taylor, Sandra Anne. *The Hidden Power of Your Past Lives.*

Van Praagh, James. *Adventures of the Soul.*

Virtue, Doreen. *Angel Therapy.*

Virtue, Doreen. *Angel Therapy Handbook.*

Virtue, Doreen. *Messages from Your Angels.*

Virtue, Doreen, and James Van Praagh. *How to Heal a Grieving Heart.*

Weiss, Brian. *Messages from the Masters.*

Weiss, Brian. *Mirrors of Time.*

Weiss, Brian. *Miracles Happen.*

Weiss, Brian. *Only Love Is Real.*

Weiss, Brian. *Through Time into Healing.*

www.BelindaWomack.com.

www.eraofpeace.com.

www.lonerwolf.com.

Printed in the United States
By Bookmasters